"SLAUGHTER US ALL AND MAKE OUR BLOOD A RIVER..."

Cyprus Poetry and History

BASED ON VASILIS MICHAELIDES POEM

"9TH OF JULY 1821, IN NICOSIA, CYPRUS".

TRANSLATION, HISTORY AND COMMENTARY

BY ANDREAS ANTONIOU MELAS

Dedicated to the memory of my father, Cyprus poet and writer Tonis Melas, and my late brother Rolandos Melas.

ISBN-13: 978-1514853313

ISBN-10: 1514853310

Author contact: threehellenecypriots@gmail.com

Cover design support by: Sean Harvey Design

Printed by CreateSpace an Amazon.com Company

TABLE OF CONTENTS

LIST OF FIGURES

INSPIRATION

Rivers of blood flowed many a time after a conquering army took over an unfortunate enemy city or town. Do we though, ever hear of anyone voluntarily agreeing to being slaughtered? No, and for obvious good reason. Yet, on July 9, 1821 the Greek Orthodox Archbishop of Cyprus offered, apparently, such an agreement. Just why would he do that? And sounding so steadfast about it? How did that happen? Let us think Christ like and read on!

Recently we have heard or seen reports of innocent Christians and others, being executed, even beheaded by Muslin fanatics for no reason other than their faith. Such a barbaric act is not something new to the people of Cyprus, the eastern Mediterranean island country. Throughout Cyprus' long history its people suffered repeatedly under foreign conquerors. Christianity took hold in Cyprus when in 43 A.D it became the first state governed by a Christian. The Roman Governor (proconsul) Sergius Paulus, accepted Christianity through Apostle Paul.

In 1821 the Christian Orthodox Church leaders along with many other local leaders, were brutally executed by the Ottoman Turkish island governor (see reference #1). The event of the executions is well documented by modern Greek historian Spyridon Trikoupis (see reference #2). In another work on these events of July 9, 1821, also written in Greek, George Kypiadou lays out the history of what happened (See reference #3). A well deserved special mention to Tefkros Symeonides for uploading online sections from the Kypiadou reference.

Nearly a century later, a native Greek Cypriot poet, Vasilis Michaelides, wrote the epic poem on the events leading to the execution (see reference #4). I found the Kypiadou reference very useful to better understand the poem. The poet, Vasilis Michaelides, used the events more or less as prescribed in the Kypiadou book, developed the main characters, added drama through the dialogue and comments and brought it to life. He wrote eloquently and more importantly, he pointed out that it is the fanatics who are doomed.

It is also important, in my view, to showcase this poem as a significant example of native Cyprus literature worth reading by the English speaking and Christian world. To the best of my knowledge, the entire poem was not previously translated into English, although short portions were (see reference #5).

Figure1. Painting "Archbishop Kyprianos and the Turkish governor in the Sarayion", Archbishopric library, Nicosia, Cyprus.

BACKGROUND

Vasilis Michaelides

Vasilis Michaelides is considered Cyprus' national poet. He composed this particular poem in the last part of the nineteenth century. At that time, 1878 actually, Cyprus came under British Empire control. Under the harsh Turkish Ottoman rule it was simply not possible to have such a poem published. Yet, the details of the brutal executions of July 1821 were passed down the generations until the poet found out and was inspired to compose this poem (see Reference #4). The poem was published in 1911, in Limassol, Cyprus, then under Mayor Christodoulos Sozos able leadership (See Reference #13).

Epic Poetry

This poem is often referred to as epic. However, a closer examination according to what is indicated in the Simple English Wikipedia, shown below, reveals some differences (shown in underlined text). That is:

Epics have six main characteristics:
1. The hero is outstanding. ...
This poem: Yes in this case too, although the villain is repugnant.
2. The setting is large. ...
Yes and No. it takes place in confined city quarters.
3. The action is made of deeds of great valor or requiring superhuman courage.
Yes, the hero's self sacrifice is valiant.
4. Supernatural forces—gods, angels, demons—insert themselves in the action.
No supernatural forces.

5. It is written in a very special style.
Yes, in fifteen syllable iambic form and Cypriot Greek
6. The poet tries to remain objective.
Yes, he does, presenting both good and evil Turks.

The poem

The poem comprises of fifty six verses, each with ten lines. It is composed in fifteen syllable iambic form, a poetic form that dates to the 10th Century. In this form we find that each line consists of fifteen syllables. The even syllables are accented while the odd syllables are not. Thus the last word of each line is accented on the second from the end syllable. Furthermore, each line contains two parts, the first one with the first eight and the second with the remaining seven syllables. When the poem is recited, a short breadth is taken after the first eight syllable half. Each line expresses a complete meaning, where the second half repeats the meaning expressed in the first half.

The use of this form is not unexpected since Greeks settled in Cyprus and maintained their language and culture over the millennia. It is considered epic as it narrates the events but also the battle of the minds between the Greek and the Turkish leader. While the Turkish leader expresses his wish to slaughter the entire Cypriot Greek population, the Archbishop wants to have only his life taken to prevent this total annihilation of his flock. One must read the entire poem to find out how all this settles out.

The poem is written in the Cyprus spoken language. This spoken language is basically ancient Greek (including words from

Homeric to classical, to koine and New Testament Greek) that has been corrupted by the various Cyprus' conqueror languages of the past millennium, that is, Frankish, Venetian, Turkish and English. As such, the poem represents the Cypriot literature which has not been recognized as a separate one until recently.

The poem has not been widely recognized outside of Cyprus itself for its beauty, poetic value and multiple messages. It is characterized by the dramatization of events and the insight in the human psyche and condition such as self sacrifice, greatness, leadership, compassion but also naiveté, deception, brutality, pursuit of power and financial gain and just plain evil.

The poet portrays winds gathering clouds and becoming a storm in Turkey but unnoticed in Cyprus ("secret winds", literally), as the harbinger of bad things to come. The events are taking place in July when a rainstorm in Cyprus was not and has not been at all common and as such it is considered a bad omen.

The poet is open minded, as he portrays the decency and goodness of Turkish high officials, who on five occasions (read in the poem) tried in vain to save the Cyprus archbishop's life. Indeed one feels a lot of respect for Kkioroglou, the Turkish official and wonders whether he existed and acted as in the poem. According to Kypiadou (Reference #3, page 14) Kkioroglou did indeed exist, although Kypiadou did not indicate any action by him as in the poem. Kkioroglou was the Nicosia leader of the Janissary force there. Certainly, that could explain quite a lot of his behavior, if that indeed happened as in the poem. As is well known, the Janissaries were fierce Ottoman fighters, who as Christian boys were forcibly taken and trained

9

to be loyal fighters for the Sultan. It is conceivable Kkioroglou remembered his Christian roots, had pity on the Archbishop, and stood up to the Turkish governor without fear. Kkioroglou's son as per poem, confirmed that possibility.

The poet also demonstrates the evil of the highest Turkish official in Cyprus named Küçük Mehmet and the order from the Sultan to execute so many innocent Greek Cypriots on suspicion alone. As per Kypiadou reference, Küçük Mehmet was motivated not only by power but also by financial gain. As per order of execution, all of the properties of the branded dissenters would be auctioned off very cheaply and typically go to the high Ottoman Turkish officials. In the poem, he not only appears fearsome, but also sweet to the slow witted shepherd, cunning and decisive to execute all of the bishops. Kypiadou indicates that this Cyprus governor, after his tenure there, was promoted to be the Ottoman Empire Chief of Police, a very important post.

Interestingly, and if indeed it was the case, the often indicated cause by the Turks to save the Archbishop was mere pity, not moral indignation, nor rebelling against unjust authority. Another important factor that may have motivated the Turkish leaders to aid the Archbishop was the fact that many Muslims in Cyprus were Christians of Cyprus who had earlier converted to Islam but maintained a secret connection with Christianity. This phenomenon of crypto Christians is well documented (see Reference #6). They did this to survive and to lead a better life, as only Muslims were allowed to own land as well as enjoy other privileges that we take for granted today. We have much evidence of this phenomenon in that many villages with

Christian names had residents who spoke Greek but were recorded officially as Muslims. Many of these Muslims voluntarily petitioned at the end of the nineteenth century the new authorities to return to Christianity. This indeed happened once Cyprus came under the British Empire, that is, after 1878 (See reference #7).

Cyprus Orthodox Church Archbishop Kyprianos was a strong, pragmatic and wise leader of his people (see Reference 8).The Archbishop's valiant stand was shown not only to be wise but more significantly, one of self sacrifice to save his people. It is also clear the Archbishop was aware of his coming demise, as written by an English visitor to the island. At the same time, as seen in Reference #3, a Greek Cypriot cleric did distribute war leaflets around the island. This is also mentioned in the poem as the cause for the Ottoman Turkish Sultan to sign the death sentences of the nearly five hundred leaders. Let us reflect on the freedom of speech and due process we enjoy now.

The poet also shows great insight into the strategic considerations on Cyprus, Greece and Turkey. Very perceptive by the poet is the realization of Cyprus' precarious geographical position, being very close to Turkey while at a large distance from Greece. That meant Cypriot Greeks were not well nor timely informed of what was happening outside the island. The evidence is in the poem, such as about the winds blowing in Turkey but unnoticed in Cyprus, as well as events in mainland Greece such as the beginning of the revolution (see verse 1). The poet through the Turkish governor confirms that is so in the poem, as he describes the Greek Cypriots as "lambs in a separate barn" from mainland Greeks (see verse 51).

See also Reference 9 for a scholarly perspective.

The poem may be divided into nine sections, as follows:

1. The set up for the coming atrocity, verses 1 and 2.

2. The Turkish official Kkioroglou tries to convince the Archbishop to leave to save himself, verses 2 to 7

3. The arrest of the Archbishop, verses 8 to 12

4. Initial face off between the Archbishop and the Ottoman Turkish governor, verses 13 to 21.

5. False confession extracted from the shepherd, verses 22 to 29.

6. All the bishops are now in jail and new efforts by Kkioroglou and another Turkish official to save the Archbishop's life, verses 30 to 40.

7. Final face off between the Archbishop and Ottoman Turkish Governor, verses 41 to 47.

8. Final effort by Kkioroglou to save the Archbishop's life, verses 48 to 52.

9. The Archbishop's hanging and the beheading of the three bishops and the shepherd, verses 53 to 56.

WARNING: VERSE #55 IS RATHER GRAPHIC

HISTORICAL BACKGROUND

We can only be certain of some of the details of what happened on that fateful day of July 9, 1821 in Nicosia, Cyprus. We can not be certain of what was so vividly said (or not) and portrayed with such detail in words and emotions by the poet.

We know that by this time, the Greek Revolution in mainland Greece had taken hold. The Greek Orthodox Patriarch in Constantinople, today's Istanbul, Gregory V, was hung on Easter Sunday 1821 from the gate of the church where he presided by the Turks. The Greek Orthodox Patriarch in Constantinople is Orthodox Christianity's leader and first among equals of the various Orthodox Christian churches. According to the governing system (Shari' a law) of the Ottoman Turks, the Greek Orthodox leader was held responsible and had to pay with his life. Indeed many Greek Orthodox Church leaders were executed by the Ottoman Turks and a major pogrom took place in Constantinople in 1821 (See Reference #10).

We can expect that the Ottoman Turks were afraid the mainland Greece rebellion spreading to surround them and were willing to take harsh pre emptive measures. The Turkish officials could also realize economic benefits by taking the possessions of the as branded dissenting Greek Cypriots, for themselves. So they managed by deception to gather within Nicosia four hundred and eighty six Greek Cypriot leaders. The Turks then locked the city and all those Greek Cypriot who did not convert to Islam (reportedly thirteen) were slaughtered either by hanging or by decapitation. Before the archbishop was hung, as in the poem, he gave the arrogant and blood thirsty Turkish official the often

13

quoted response that killing him was not the end and that it was in vain. According to the poem, but also as per Reference #3, the Turkish officials forced a naïve shepherd to make a false confession that the Greek Cypriot church leaders were fostering a coup against them. Cyprus at that time was not heavily populated with a total of less than one hundred thousand people, a small fraction of what it is today. The native Greek Cypriots had no army, no navy and no military tradition, thus unable to protect themselves from outside aggressors.

The bodies of the hung archbishop and beheaded bishops were later buried in the yard of the Greek Orthodox church in Nicosia "Panayia tis Faneromenis" or " Mother of God who revealed herself ". It was from this church that in October 1931 the presiding priest declared union with Greece. That declaration began a rowdy uprising by unarmed Greek Cypriots, this time against the British Empire yoke. The first Prime Minister of post revolution Greece, Ioannis Kapodistria, acknowledged this particular shedding of Greek Cypriot blood in 1821 that it qualified Cyprus to be a part of the Modern Greek State (See reference 13, page 20).

TURKISH AGGRESSION IN CYPRUS:
THE 1570-1 A.D ATTACK AND CONQUEST TO
THE 1821 A.D SLAUGHTER TO
THE 1974 A.D INVASION AND OCCUPATION OF PART OF CYPRUS
AND THE 2014 A.D EEZ EVENTS

Cyprus, owing to its strategic location at the intersection of three continents, has been subjugated by the regional superpowers throughout its long history and more recently by a global superpower. Greeks (Hellenes) settled on the island starting around 1600 B.C. Yet, throughout the millennia the Greek character and civilization of the island was not extinguished despite all the foreign power interferences. More information on Cyprus history may be found in reference #13.

After the Ottoman Turks conquered Constantinople (today's Istanbul) in 1453, they became the Muslim world's leading power. During the 1500's the Ottoman Turks sought to control all of the Mediterranean Sea. So, in 1521 they began the drive to control the Mediterranean. First, they laid siege and conquered the island of Rhodes. The 1565 siege of the island of Malta is noteworthy not only that a huge Ottoman Turkish force failed to defeat the Christian defenders, but that it turned the tide. At that time, in the eastern Mediterranean both Crete and Cyprus were still under Venetian control. Both islands were wealthy but also militarily unsupportable from Venice. Both islands were conquered by the Ottoman Turks, Cyprus in 1571 and Crete a century later.

In 1570 A.D Cyprus was attacked by Ottoman Turkey and conquered after more than a year of fierce fighting. The Cyprus defenders fought valiantly against a huge army and navy and inflicted heavy losses. Upon surrender to the Ottoman Turkish commander, the Venetian commander Marco Antonio Bragadin, was flayed alive and countless others were executed (see reference 12). Following the Cyprus conquest, the Ottoman Turks eliminated most of the Latin Christians there.

At the same time, the Ottoman Turks conquerors allowed the Greek Cypriots and the Greek Orthodox Church, some measure of freedom, as long as they were compliant, paid their taxes and did not rebel. Yet, during the 17th Century we have accounts of the island population dropping to between thirty and fifty thousand or about 3 to 5% of what it is today (see Reference 13). That population decline contributed to a subdued Greek Cypriot population and no major revolts over three centuries. In fact Kypiadou reports that once the Greek Revolution begun and the Ottoman Sultan reacted, he sent a very mild letter to Cyprus ordering disarmament and praising the cooperation of Cypriots to Ottoman rulers.

In 1821, as a Greek mainland revolution was taking hold, the Cyprus Greek Orthodox Archbishop Kyprianos was encouraging no dissent whatsoever against Ottoman Turkey. The Archbishop encouraged the Greek Cypriots to a peaceful disarmament which was carried out without any dissent. Unfortunately, a Greek cleric came over to the island and distributed war related papers. For that the Archbishop was held accountable and was hung. Along with him were nearly five hundred clergy and local leaders. Nearly all were slaughtered over a six day period in July 1821. Following this massacre, much more aggression took place by a large Turkish army already brought in from outside of Cyprus.

In 1878, Cyprus, by a turn of events, was handed to the British Empire to pay for the Ottoman Turkish debts incurred in the 1850's Crimean war. The new rule resulted in a significant improvement in the lives of Cypriots. Yet, in 1950 they peacefully demanded through a referendum, self determination from their British Empire masters. When that demand failed, they conducted a successful guerilla style revolt. The British Empire masters then escalated their actions to foment friction in the relations between the local Greek and Turkish communities. After Cyprus became independent in 1960, the Greek and Turkish Cypriots went through further inter communal friction. Finally, in 1974, Turkey invaded and occupies to now, a major portion of the island. The Turks acted with the same brutality and malicious behavior in 1974 as they did in 1571 and 1821.

Among the highlights of the 1974 Turkish aggression against Cyprus: 1. Very large in numbers and proportion to population, forced movements of both Greek and Turkish Cypriots away from their homes. A total of over 200,000 people or approximately 40% of the population became refugees in their own country. Creation of two separate areas by a huge Turkish armed force. This continues to now.

2. Large numbers of killings, rapes and other atrocities by the Turkish armed forces. Over 1500 Greek Cypriots still missing.

3. Nearly six hundred Greek Orthodox Churches abandoned by force. This was followed by the conversion of large numbers of these churches into other uses and abuses.

4. Large numbers of mainland Turkey settlers brought in the northern and occupied area, creating additional tensions on the Turkish Cypriots and forcing many to leave the island.

This aggressive stance of Turkey against the Greek Cypriots was exemplified once again in late 2014. As potentially large hydrocarbon deposits were found in the Exclusive Economic Zone (EEZ) of Cyprus, Turkey sent its own oil exploration vessel named Barbaros escorted by naval boats. Interestingly, Barbaros is an apt name for such a barbaric act. Turkey did so despite international condemnation and protests. Turkey does not recognize the sovereignty of the Republic of Cyprus and does not recognize the EEZ of any island country such as Cyprus. As Turkey is extremely strong militarily it can bully its way on a small island nation such as Cyprus and it does.

It is noted in the poem that the atrocities are conceived in Turkey with the support and by the instigation of a small number in the Turkish Cypriot leadership. Then, they are carried out against the unprotected Greek Cypriot population, by Turks brought in from Turkey itself. Back in 1821 and again in 1974, Turkish Cypriots, anecdotally, showed compassion and protected their Greek Cypriot neighbors from mainland Turk atrocities. On both occasions the local average Turks had no power to shape events, as the Turkish military and a small group of Turkish Cypriot leaders had the upper hand. The fact remains, no difference in the way the Turkish side treated Greek Cypriots and other Christians, be it during Ottoman times or recently by the modern Turkish State.

THE TRANSLATION

In this work, my emphasis was to portray the meaning of what is in the original locally spoken Greek Cypriot dialect (which is hard to do unless one grows up with it), to what is standard American English, rather than consistently engaging in literal word translation. As a spoken language that does not have symbols for every sound and no standardized words in their writing form, it becomes even trickier to know what is written. The poet Vasilis Michaelides not only used the locally spoken Cypriot Greek, he also coined words, which made the translation even more difficult. In any case, I am confident I am expressing the meaning of the original poem as faithfully as possible, so that English speaking persons may have the most correct and accurate understanding of what is said in the poem.

Some words need explanation:

1. Lefcosia is the Greek name for the capital city of Nicosia. At the time of the poem it was a walled city built from the period Cyprus was under the Latins, first Franks and then Venetians, that is since the 1200's.

2. Romioi and Romious is the term Greek Orthodox Christians used to call themselves, and Romiosini is the whole Greek Orthodox race. This term is derived from the East Roman Empire, later named Byzantium, which was both Christian and Greek.

3. Sarayion was the Turkish Cyprus Governor's palace, inside the then walled city of Nicosia. It was built by the Frankish kings of Cyprus in an earlier period. Now it is situated in the Turkish controlled area of Nicosia.

4. The Turkish Cyprus Governor's name was Küçük Mehmet but referred to in the poem as Mousellim-Aga, that is, Muslim Leader. The Turkish leaders were called Aga.

5. Millet was in the Ottoman Turkish administrative system, a surrogate unit of governing comprised of people associated by religion and or ethnic ties. The leader was accountable to the local Turkish leader. The Greek Orthodox hierarch was also called Ethnarch and accountable to the Ottoman Turkish leader.

6. The High Porte was the seat of power in the Ottoman Empire, where decisions were made. The Sultan along with the Grand Vizier were the highest two officials.

7. Skala, modern Larnaca, is a coastal city in Cyprus, which owing to its proximity to the capital Nicosia had a number of foreign consulates during this period. Foreign diplomats provided third person accounts of the various events that corroborated the persecution of Greek Orthodox Christians in Cyprus.

8. The poet used certain Cyprus countryside areas (Pitsillous, and Malounta) to describe the headsman and the shepherd.

9. Karamania is a province in southern Turkey facing Cyprus.

10. Mesir, indicated as Mesirin in the poem, is the Arabic name for Egypt.

With all of the above introduction and background material in mind, let us proceed to the high drama of the translated poem. **Be warned that Verse 55 is rather graphic on the execution details.**

The reader may find it worthwhile as I did, to search for the quotable quotes, which are numerous.

1

Even as in Turkey the winds silently grew stronger,
bringing in the clouds and changing the sky
and the clouds continuing to gather from all directions
until they filled the sky so thickly, they created the storm,
in Cyprus it was calm, though Cyprus had its secrets too,
in the winds blowing unnoticed, Cyprus had its share of woes too.
While the lightning that appeared in the Morias (Greece)
spread and its thunder was heard everywhere,
and all was lit up, all the seas and all the lands,
in Cyprus it was calm, though it too had its share of the evil to come.

2

It was a quiet night, in the month of July,
a Friday night it was, when millions of stars
were shining from above, yet no one was wondering
around the narrow streets and turns of Nicosia,
no wind blowing, not even a tree leaf was moving,
not even a dog's bark, nor a cock's crow were heard,
it was a quiet night, a depressing night,
that made you think it was hiding from God's judgment.
In such a quiet night the Turkish leaders locked inside
the Sarayion were holding a great council.

3

It was past midnight and towards sunrise
when Kkioroglou, who had a good, a really good heart,
secretly left his house and went to the Archbishop's,
where he woke up the Archbishop, sat next to him and told him:
"Kyprianos, my horse carriage is ready at my house,
my carriage is in place and ready to go, Kyprianos,
and if you want to avoid certain hanging
and if you want from certain death to get away,
you can go along with my harem to Skala,
where the consulates are open for you to hide.

4

Mousellim-aga received orders from the Porte,
so last night suddenly, there was a council,
and he has the authority to deal death to you,
it is in his hands to judge you, to give you death.
Do not delay Kyprianos, do not lose time,
go and disappear if you know what's good for you.
You must go, because if you do not, without a doubt,
if sunrise comes and you are still here,
you will hang dead, or dead on the stake.
Get up and let us go quickly the carriage is waiting."

5

Kyprianos looked down for a little while
and as he was somewhat tempted says:
"I do not wish, Kkioroglou, to leave the city,
because, if I do, the disaster will be even worse.
I choose to stay, even as they will kill me,
let them kill me so that others will survive.
I am not leaving, because my departure
will bring certain death to the Romious of this land.
I will be putting the rope around the neck of my people;
Better to shed the Bishop's blood, instead of so many others."

6

Kkioroglou then repeats:" I feel sorry for you, Bishop,
because if sunrise finds you in this city,
your head will be the first to fall.
A big dark man left an hour ago,
and climbed over the wall and into the street,
and is going to Larnaca, to the foreign consulates.
They brought for him and he wore a suit like those
of the Pitsillous, raggedy, ugly, mixed up
and raggedy, raggedy boots on his legs,
in case anyone recognizes him in the street".

7

"Thank you, Kkioroglou", said the Archbishop
"I can see your mother's milk was good,
but leave now before they see you and brand you a traitor."
Kkioroglou then said: "if you do not want to be afar,
let us go to my house, do not stay here".
"I wish to stay, Kkioroglou, even if I die."
Kkioroglou was trying hard to do a good deed,
but all his efforts were in vain.
Time was running out and he should not stay there,
so he left sorrowful and regretful.

8

The night was getting even shorter,
the east was turning more reddish yellow,
as it became that bitter Saturday morning,
and then the wooden bell was heard.
Kyprianos went outside bearing his pain,
and went into the church and made the sign of the cross
and that he did as the church liturgy begun,
and he stood full of sorrow and as he was almost tempted,
he went and knelt before the icon of the Virgin Mary
and he mumbled something and started crying.

9

He stood still, he did not move, as if he was nailed there,
kneeling, afflicted and with his arms crossed,
he got up only when the holy communion was given out,
and as he stood there with tears in his eyes,
he adored the Virgin Mary icon three or four times,
as if he was saying goodbye to the world and people.
He asked for forgiveness by all and went inside the Holy Altar,
and there he received communion and then he stood there,
looking like he was dead, about to be buried,
you would think he lost all his blood.

10

He came out of the church along with his followers,
and immediately was surrounded by Sarayion Turks.
He gave them right away a terrifying look
as his eye brows were showing his anger.
They stood there stunned at his anger
as if their mouths were shut tight.
 So he asked: "Who sent you so early this morning?
Tell me, speak up and do not hesitate,
and in case you pity me, my heart is like a rock,
tell me what you want, do not feel embarrassed.

11

"We came to arrest you, we are on orders
by Mousellim-aga the governor of this land"
He said:" if you were milk fed well,
stop, wait for me for five minutes"
(and who knew what he was hiding inside of him!).
He left in a hurry and went to his quarters
and lit a candle and put some papers on fire
and then he turned and said "let us go men,
now that I finished my affairs as I wish,
take me and we go as you were ordered to do.

12

Take me, to put me, an innocent man, to my death,
take me, put me to death for no reason at all".
So, with some to his right, others left, back and front,
surrounded he was, they went on their way.
Mousellim was sitting with the other high officers
in the Sarayion and said to the other Bishops:
" I heard the three of you and your millet leader
along with the leaders and the wealthy here
promised to the Romious, on your life,
to not let Romious remain slaves any longer"

13

Even as he was still not finished speaking,
the Turks brought the Archbishop to him.
He indicated with the turn and nod of his face
to one of the swordsmen to come near him,
and he leaned over and said in his ear: "In two minutes
close shut all three doors of the city,
lest the Romioi escape and go to the mountains to hide.
Outside Sarayion keep the crowds away,
inside Sarayion all (the Turks) to be doubled armed,
and the armed men and the headsmen ready on the double.

14

Then he turns and says to the Archbishop,
leaning down, his eye brows crossed and looking horrible:
" Archbishop Kyprianos, millet leader of the island,
I wanted to tell you I have my orders
from the Porte and have the sealed order,
I have an important order from the High See
the wealthy Romious, the leaders of this land
to gather them all and execute them immediately,
not to spare even one, not even a bishop,
to put them all to death any way I choose."

15

He said: "Mousellim-aga, the good Muslim that you are,
you have in your hands the order from on high
and you have such an order, how can you do otherwise?
Do as you are ordered to do from the high See
burn us, hang us or cut our heads off,
we only ask you to tell us what our offense is."
" You were agitating to join with the other Romious,
to fight the Turks from all four sides,
you too were arming yourselves to start a rebellion,
all of you to join together to defeat the Turks."

16

"We do not know of anyone who arrived on this island
and who secretly brought arms so that you can falsely accuse us.
We surrendered our arms, all of us, young and old,
and as soon as you ordered us to turn in those arms.
For what reason could we pick up arms now
and join with others to fight against you?
Who ever said these words to you in your ears,
even if he is a Christian, he must hate us,
he must be fighting us, all because of his jealousy,
we say to you, these accusations are false, we are innocent."

17

" Do not deny this, you bishops and monks,
you sent people to the villages to pass out papers,
that all Romioi arm themselves and stand ready
as soon as they get your word to start slaughtering us,
and I do not believe whatever someone says,
but I have some of the papers, can you still argue?"
He says:" Mousellim-aga, I said and keep saying to you:
regarding all these accusations our conscious is clean,
believe me, if not, the offense is on your head,
this job clearly happened without our knowledge."

18

'"Bishop, you can be certain, I never change my views,
no matter what you say, do not expect that I will believe you.
I made up my mind, bishop, to slaughter and to hang,
and if I could, I would kill all Romious in Cyprus,
and even more, if I could go all over the whole world,
I would slaughter all Romious, not leave one alive."
"The Romiosini is as old as Creation;
no one has managed to eliminate us,
no one, because my God is protecting us from on high.
Romiosini, will only vanish when the world comes to the end.

19

Slaughter us all and make our blood a river,
slaughter all our people and kill the Romioi like goats,
but beware, when the aging poplar is cut,
three hundred seedlings sprout around it.
The plow emboldened as it tills, feels it is indestructible,
but it is always the plow that is worn, the plow that is ruined.
You are so bitter inside of you, but if you must slaughter,
slaughter those who are armed and somewhere else.
Why hurt us, our hands are clean,
we have no arms and have been absolutely obedient."

20

At that moment Mousellim lifted up his eyes,
and looked at him sweetly, and opens up to him and says:
" Whatever a man suffers comes from inside his head,
the submissive man looses his life by the sword,
and you too, if you are submissive, you are loosing your life."
" Stop talking, I knew this already, before you started talking,
stop trying to dry up the sea.
You are wasting words, in vain you are delaying your job.
Can you put out the sun with a puff of breath alone?
Call your hangman, prepare the gallows for our hanging!"

21

Mousellim and all the Turks around him, as they heard this,
looked like a thunderbolt struck them:
They all stopped talking and were looking at one another,
each one was trying to hide their shame.
Mousellim then realized he was wasting his efforts,
and ordered to move the bishops away from him,
and they took them to the jail without separating them.
The Turks, now by themselves, turned to planning the evil
and they decided to bring in witnesses
so they brought a slow witted shepherd from Malounta.

22

Mousellim says: "Dimitri, do not be afraid,
because I see you as one of my own men.
What is it that you want; just tell me and do not be tempted."
" I only ask, my Lord, to go to my village,
since you kept me locked inside the city,
my herd is all over the mountain side
let me out for two days and take my soul afterwards,
I only want to know what happened to my flock,
I will come back and even on my return,
I will be back with a handshake and a goat for you.

23

I do not have, my Lord, an assistant or a servant,
and was told my goats are dying from hunger.
I only had one son in my family,
and have been without him for a month now.
One Sunday, when we were together, he and I,
and were catching birds with the sticky sticks,
I offered him to go and join those in the war march,
and he went but did not return, may that day be on fire.
They told me they left from the Karpas peninsula
with a group of locals, who went further away,

24

where the young are fighting, and towards Constantinople.
If they are fighting for a good cause and my son with them,
I accept if he is lost for God, if he dies from a bullet,
even if I am left alone to live without him.
But if they are fighting to make trouble,
may their mother's milk be for shame.
It has been a while since my son left me,
I am all alone to handle the herd,
I sleep and wake up alone,
and alone I stand by the watering hole to water.

25

In this condition, my Lord, how much longer can I remain?
Melancholy has made taken over me,
because eating, eats me, drinking, melts me,
my grief is so big, my heart is burning.
I used to wake up at dawn, to go to wash,
and was always singing,
and felt the whole world was singing with me,
and was making people mad at me day and night,
and played my flute and the mountains were singing,
my eyes did not know grief nor tears.

26

"I will allow you" he said "to go to your village,
and will forgive all your taxes as long as you live,
and if you have debts I will pay those for you,
and will even count in your palms one hundred gold coins.
You said your bishops wanted to see you rebel
to have the Christians slaughter the Turks.
You said your bishops, even the children,
the young men and the old and the women also,
were taking up arms and bullets and gun powder,
and others heard this as I did from your own mouth."

27

"As for me, my Lord, I only heard others say,
that a local monk came from over there,
and be brought a bunch of papers from the war front
and as soon as he passed them out he disappeared,
and all those papers were about the war.
Everything else you said, I never did hear."
" Why are you lying to me, are we your servants?
You said it with your own words, in your own story,
say it, or else I kill you, I cut your head off.
Bring the headsman, to stand here, and be ready!"

28

"No, my Lord, do not spill blood on me.
Pity me, the unfortunate, it is a pity and a sin,
let me say it: yes it is true, my Lord,
(fear brings hell, as the saying goes)
I will change the bitter to sweet and the twisted into straight
and I will say as you wish, my Lord, in order to escape.
What you said is true, my Lord, I bear witness,
I saw it with my own eyes, I heard with my own ears,
it all happened, I saw it all, I say it and say it again.
My God forgive me, my heart is clean."

29

The shepherd said all this and cried uncontrollably.
The Turks then spoke into each other's ears
and put on a paper the shepherd's confession,
(and who knew that really what the confession said)
and they brought it to poor Dimitri and he touched it,
and he put his finger print on it and sealed it that way.
Mousellim then spoke to him sweetly,
and said to him:" Stop crying and I will release you."
he gave him a sweet look and smiled at him
and gave the order to take him away to the back.

30

Then they were talking to each other for some time,
about those to be killed and opened a book
to see who were from the countryside and who from the city
and how many to hang and how many to knife.
And there were five or six who said "too many, it is a pity",
and Mousellim said "all of them are to die!"
The sun by now was up high, it was noon
and the Muslim prayer was called from the minaret
and they stopped talking and left the book there
and all went to noon prayer gathering.

31

The prison was dark and small,
where the four bishops were sitting alone,
and had on the side of the garden an iron door,
and their talk with soft voices was heard.
Bishop Laurentios said:" Oh, the blessed one,
God protected, but also arrogant!
he brought those bad papers and without thinking
he filled the island all over,
and gave them everywhere he went
and now they came back to haunt us."

32

Bishop Meletios says: "I hate injustice.
This man tried to do a good deed,
how can we blame him, that he was the cause?
It was God's will and that is what happened.
No one ever says Charon is to fault,
they always blame the deceased."
Then Kyprianos says: "These are all words in vain,
one way or another we are finished, we are lost,
any way it happened God knows from on high,
we should only care about those who remain."

33

At that moment the garden door creaked opened
and a handsome, tall and well dressed young man came in
who looked joyful and seemed to come from an aristocratic family,
but he was breathing heavy, like he was over exerted.
He was holding a clean bag under his arms,
and he went to Kyprianos and told him, speaking fast:
"My father sent me and I came running
and I brought for you a set of clothes for you to put on,
so the two of us go to our house, secretly and hiding,
so, get dressed quickly, do not delay."

34

"My son, who is your father, say his name to me so that I know."
"My father is Kkioroglou, and he told me to hurry,
to find you quickly and to bring these clothes to you,
and to bring you to our house right away, not to leave you here.
Get dressed and we go and hope God is on our side,
my father is at our house and he is waiting for us.
We will run through the garden while hiding,
and after we climb over the wall, we take the road
and if as we go we get into trouble,
if they say anything, I will cut them up in pieces."

35

"My son go and tell him to continue to do his duties,
as for me, I am just fine here where I am,
and his kindness and his good heart,
even when I am hang I will remember.
Give him my heartfelt regards and tell him even more,
that I will thank him even when I am dead and buried,
if he does an even greater kindness:
In our land from now on to do all he can
no greater injustice happens to Romiosini.
Tell him all this and may God grant him many years."

36

" I too will stand up for all these things you said
and will keep your words deep inside my soul,
and I vow to keep my faith and I will not forget,
but returning to my father without you, I am embarrassed."
At the same time from the other door a noise was heard
and they saw the locket to turn,
and the young man immediately arose
and in his hands he had the pistol,
he became angry and then cooled down,
and he took a big jump and landed in the garden.

37

The door then opened all the way,
and a Turkish leader dressed nobly came in
and said to them:" I came to see you, to talk with you,
because I fell very sad with your predicament.
I brought some food and drink for you to have,
because they will be looking for you pretty soon.
I ran and saw three gallows ready to use,
the two were from the Plane tree and the other one
from the sycamore tree and all three were like death
and I felt terrible and I lost my strength.

38

I came to tell you and to comfort you
that I will push today, I will do all that I can,
I will take down the gallows and give you a break,
and the papers they wrote I will tear up,
I will turn the sour sweet and the wild to tame
and the orders reversed to save you.
Four pillars like you, four leaders of this land,
is it not a pity for you to hang?
Of all things, life is the sweetest of all
only a word from you and you will be saved."

39

Then the Archbishop stood up
and said to him:" Turk, stop talking now,
I do not wish to hear any more words from you.
Stop, it is a pity and your words are in vain,
just go quickly and return to your duties,
death is sweeter than talking to you."
When the Turk heard this he stopped
and realized his words were in vain,
and both sad and embarrassed
he left there with sadness in his stride.

40

As soon as this Turk left and they were all alone,
all on bended knees they prayed,
and they were all sobbing and their prayer
was from inside their heart, they were in pain.
After their prayer, still on bended knees,
they said as they were sobbing in broken voices:
" Our God forgive those who hate us,
Our God free our unlucky race,
Our God give strength to those who fight,
Our God, forgive us and accept our soul!"

41

The others who were at the mosque, as they finished,
they stood up and stopped talking to each other
and in the Sarayion they gathered together
and went about to finish the job they started.
And just to spite Kyprianos and to scare him
they bring his assistant and his secretary
and accused them of wrong doing,
and hang them while their hands were tied back
from the two gallows on the plane tree,
and they left them there hanging.

42

After that they sent a dozen men from the Sarayion
and asked them to double arm themselves,
and brought out the four bishops from the jail
and all said to the bishops, in one voice,
for the very last time, they were doomed.
At that moment Mousellim says to them:
" The headsman and the hangman are both ready,
your time has come and I will not delay,
I have a new order, this time from the Vizier."
Then the Archbishop opens his mouth and says to him:

43

"Slaughter us all and record our death.
Beware though, all these killings will come back to haunt you,
you feel you dug up our own tomb,
but you do not get it, it is your own tomb you dug.
You are making things worse, as I see it,
in Constantinople you first hung the Patriarch,
and after him many bishops and priests.
Kill as many as you want, but it is you who will be hurt,
the bishops' blood you spill,
is the oil in the fire that will burn you."

44

Mousellim then says: "The day is almost over,
it is almost afternoon and the evening near,
I wait no longer, the job has started
I have two hung and the rest of the job must be finished.
I have your assistant and secretary,
And you too will see both of them hung in front of you.
If you have something to say for your own sake, say it,
so we can finish soon, before night falls,
as I remain patient, just in case "
" Be quiet, since it is you who wants us to tell you:

45

Hurry up, be quick and finish your mission,
order your headsmen to cut our head off,
bring your sword quickly and the rope to hang us,
so here, we said it to you, for our own good."

Mousellim then looked at them indicating terror will follow.
All of the others got up with an evil look on their faces,
they picked up the bishops as if in a rage
then quickly tied them up and took them
and stood them up still tied up, outside Sarayion.

46

At that time Mousellim said to the agas:
"Every evil man deserves death,
we are going to behead the bishops now
and in the morning will start with the leaders,
those who secretly dug up Turkey a tomb.
It is the order from the Sultan, we bear no responsibility.
It is because of their craze they and their race are suffering,
they will suffer even more with this mindset,
it is of their own doing, let it be on their own head."
Kkioroglou then gets up and says:

47

" You have your own soul to give to God, Mousellim-aga,
he who breaks his vows does evil to his soul,
the Archbishop, you vowed not to kill him,
you vowed never to have his head cut."
" I do not wish to receive advice from you, Kkioroglou.
If I break my vow it is my own doing.
When I made my vow, you were not there,
he refused and did not accept grace from me,
he told me: Mousellim-aga, if you want to give me grace,
do not hurt anyone in this land.

48

So I accepted his offer, if not, he can say
in the case I hurt a youngster or a baby,
let the sword first take my head,
and I do not accept your grace, so cut my head off first.
But, do you feel I will change my opinion?
The vow I took, I will keep that too.
I vowed never to cut his head off,
some I cut their head, others hang,
I did not vow to grant him his life,
to strangle is different from slaughter."

49

Then Kkioroglou said: "This job with the bishops,
I am afraid will bring troubles to this land,
in case the Romioi change their mind and cause trouble,
to create friction and starting now.
They may get angry and rise up,
as they see our actions and then they will not be detracted."
Then Mettes-aga says:" Put the fears aside,
we should not hurry the bishops job,
let us put it aside for five or six days,
to stretch out the job and to investigate further.

50

To investigate within the Romious to find out
in case they have more arms hidden in their houses.
And after we check and we are very certain,
we will have no worries, we will be at peace."
Mousellim then responds and says:
" I have no fear of the Cypriots,
they can see in Karamania the Turks are a multitude,
and they are so close, they can hear the dogs barking,
only a whistle and a great many Turks will come
and they can slaughter all Cypriots in just one hour.

51

On the other hand they have Misirin (Egypt) near them.
As far as ships they have none, they are farmers.
Because of all these reasons they can not get ahead,
the bishops made up their minds from the beginning,
if not, they too were looking after themselves,
and those who are fighting they too have their woes coming.
Over here these people are very far away,
months pass until they hear what happened elsewhere
and even more, they are surrounded by Turkey.
Greeks here are like lambs in a separate barn.

52

We are late, let us go now, it is afternoon now,
do not be concerned about any trouble in Cyprus,
nothing bad will happen, I am confident,
as far as this job is concerned do not be tempted."
So, then, all of them and at the same time got up
and went outside of Sarayion and stood there.
On the right side from the plane tree were the two who hung
and on the left, from the sycamore tree one gallows was ready,
and the bishops were on the earth, their hands tied together
and the Muslims were standing around them with great joy.

53

The Turks and the Cypriots were really sad looking,
as they were all quiet and tempted.
Mousellim looking quite pleased gave the order then,
and they took Kyprianos, two or three with arms,
underneath the sycamore tree, near his death site
and the rope was beating on his forehead.
Then they forced the three bishops on their knees
facing west, all three in line and in front of them
were the three headsmen looking like wild people
and they went over them as they were moving their swords.

54

Then, the Archbishop lifted up his eyes
towards heaven, and his eyes appeared to cry,
it seemed his soul was hurting from deep inside,
and he said these words, his lips burning:
" My God, whose kindness has no bounds,
pity us and give now some happiness to Romiosini."
The sweat was dripping from his face,
from the sun's rays that were so strong
and they put the rope around his neck
and there and then his suffering came to an end.

55

After that the headsmen, each with a big sword,
cut up the other three who were on bended knees
and Dimitri the shepherd, as soon as they brought him
and then the three headsmen just stood there.
The blood collected on the soil and made a puddle
and the heads and bodies were moving.
Even the Turks were saddened by this carnage,
and every person said from inside their heart, it is a pity.
Then the call to prayer from the minaret was heard,
and they left the slaughtered there and unburied.

56

After this evil act was heard around the city,
and the crying brought the people to a boil,
a short time after sunset,
when it was almost nightfall,
two leaders and four priests came
and asked Mousellim-aga:" Give us the bishops
and Dimitri too, to bury them , it is a pity not to."
And he said with a lot of anger and fearsome intimidation:
"Go away, I will give you no one to bury,
I want them where they are and unburied for three days!"

END Vassilis Michaelides' "The 9th of July 1821"as translated by Andreas Antoniou Melas, 2015, U.S.A.

Figure2. "The Hanging of Archbishop Kyprianos", 20th Century, carved in wood, Cultural Center, Archbishop Makarios III, in Nicosia, Cyprus.

EPILOGUE

The years and decades indeed almost two centuries have gone by, and even though the evil perpetrated against the Greek Orthodox Church leaders of Cyprus has been almost forgotten, the brave and Christ-like stand by the Archbishop to save his flock continues to bear fruit and three hundred rose to replace him in the fight for liberty and justice.

The danger to the people of Cyprus continues to today from Turkish aggression. Recent events such as the non recognition of the sovereignty of the Republic of Cyprus and its exclusive economic zone by Turkey are worrisome signs.

Vasilis Michaelides also wrote another poem exalting Archbishop Kyprianos. This time he wrote it in the "Katharevousa" or the Modern Greek which is closer to ancient Greek:

Τῷ ἀπαγχονισθέντι Ἀρχιεπισκόπῳ Κύπρου Κυπριανῷ:

Σὺ ποῦ σκοτώθης γιὰ τὸ φῶς σήκου νὰ δῆς τὸν ἥλιο,

ξύπνα, νὰ δεῖς τὸ αἷμα σου πῶς ἔγινε βασίλειο.

OR IN ENGLISH:

To the hung Archbishop of Cyprus Kyprianos:

You, who died to bring us the light, get up to see the sun,

wake up, look, your blood became a kingdom.

50

PERSONAL CONNECTION

Near the house where I was born in Limassol, Cyprus, there is a small park which is dedicated to Vasilis Michaelides. As a youngster, I played and passed by there countless times without much or any specific interest. As a native Greek Cypriot, I was exposed to parts of the poem since childhood. Why the interest now, then? I live some six thousand miles away and almost half a century has passed since I moved away. Certainly the recent beheadings of Christians in the Middle East by Muslim fanatics played a key role. Who can not be affected by such events? And who can forget their native land being tried once again by a powerful and at times evil neighboring country? Could this sort of event be repeated in the future?

Figure3. Vasilis Michaelides Park and bust in Limassol, Cyprus.

REFERENCES

1. 9th July 1821, Wikipedia, in Greek
http://el.wikisource.org/wiki/%CE%97_9%CE%B7_%CE%99%CE%BF%CF
%85%CE%BB%CE%AF%CE%BF%CF%85_%CF%84%CE%BF%CF%85_1821

2. "The Greek Revolution of 1821-8" by Spyridon Trikoupis, V.1

3. Γεωργίου Κηπιάδου, « Απομνημονεύματα τών κατά το 1821 Εν τr νήσω Κύπρω Τραγικών Σκηνών», OR IN ENGLISH:

George Kypiadou, « Chronicles of the 1821 in the island of Cyprus tragic events', printed in Alexandria, Egypt, 1888.

4. Vasilis Michaelides, Wikipedia, in Greek

http://el.wikipedia.org/wiki/%CE%92%CE%B1%CF%83%CE%AF%CE%BB
%CE%B7%CF%82_%CE%9C%CE%B9%CF%87%CE%B1%CE%B7%CE%BB%
CE%AF%CE%B4%CE%B7%CF%82

5. Tefkros Symeonides and Constantinos Symeonides, 1997-8.

http://www.erevos.com/enati/ninth-9.htm

6. Papademetriou, Tom, Ph.D., monograph
 "Render Unto the Sultan: Power, Authority and the Greek Orthodo⨯ Church in the Early Ottoman Centuries", published by Oxford University Press (February 2015).

7. "Linovanbakoi: Turks, Muslims or Crypto-Christians" by Fedor Papadopoulos, Ph.D., 2010 and review:
http://www.churchofcyprus.org.cy/article.php?articleID=1140

8. Kyprianos of Cyprus

http://en.wikipedia.org/wiki/Kyprianos_of_Cyprus

9. The Ecology of Coexistence and Conflict in Cyprus: Exploring the Religion ... By Irene Dietzel   Published by Walter de Gruyter GmbH & Co KG.

10. 1821 Constantinople persecution of Greeks by Ottoman Turks
http://en.wikipedia.org/wiki/Constantinople_massacre_of_1821

11. Greek Cypriots in Greek revolution of 1821, Wikipedia, in Greek

http://www.diakonima.gr/2013/01/15/%CE%BF%CE%B9-
%CE%BA%CF%8D%CF%80%CF%81%CE%B9%CE%BF%CE%B9-
%CE%B5%CE%B8%CE%B5%CE%BB%CE%BF%CE%BD%CF%84%CE%AD%
CF%82-%CF%83%CF%84%CE%B7%CE%BD-
%CE%B5%CF%80%CE%B1%CE%BD%CE%AC%CF%83%CF%84%CE%B1%C
F%83%CE%B7/

12. Marco Antonio Bragadin, Wikipedia

https://en.wikipedia.org/wiki/Marco_Antonio_Bragadin

13. Andreas Antoniou Melas "Three Hellene Cypriots" 2014, ISBN 9781497449510, paperback and ebook

ABOUT THE AUTHOR

Lemesos, Cyprus born and raised and USA University educated. He practices lifelong learning, and believes in peaceful settlement of differences among peoples.

This work follows "Three Hellene Cypriots" published in 2014.

The author, while a sixteen year old, first came to the United States. He had won an American Field Service scholarship. He made presentations about Cyprus to numerous organizations. This book is in a way an elaborate continuation, albeit at the opposite part of his life.

At Ripon College, Wisconsin, USA, he earned the A.B. degree. At Northeastern University, Boston, he continued with graduate studies earning a M.Sc. and then pursuing Ph.D. studies. Finally, he had Harvard University graduate training in Management through case studies. This gave him additional insight into policy, leadership and leaders such as those covered in this book. A rigorous Harvard writing course as well as professional writing experience helped prepare the author in this new book endeavor.

The final push in the author's decision to go through with this book was his father's example. His father, Tonis Melas, was a prolific writer and an indelible example that gave the author the "guts to go for it". Tonis Melas, in his shortened life, published nineteen books but had another thirty one ready for publication.

Figure4. Map of Cyprus after the 1974 Turkish invasion and occupation